I0811878

SIXTY-SIX BOOKS OF The Mighty Shepherd

And I Myself Will Be the Shepherd of My Sheep

ANNETTE VALENTINE

Carpenter's Son Publishing

Sixty-Six Books of the Mighty Shepherd: And I Myself Will Be the Shepherd of My Sheep
Copyright © 2024 by Annette Valentine

All rights reserved. No part of this book may be reproduced or transmitted in any form or by any means, electronic or mechanical, including photocopying, recording, or by any information storage and retrieval system, without permission in writing from the copyright owner.

Published by Carpenter's Son Publishing, Franklin, Tennessee
www.carpenterssonpublishing.com

Scripture quotations are from] New Revised Standard Version Bible, copyright © 1989 National Council of the Churches of Christ in the United States of America. Used by permission. All rights reserved worldwide.

Book edited by Robert Irvin

Book design and layout by Eve DeGrie

Author's commentary is identifiable by offset and smaller size font.

Printed in the United States of America

10 9 8 7 6 5 4 3 2 1

ISBN: 978-1-940262-43-7 (print)

Contents

Introduction

Sixty-Six Books of The Mighty Shepherd arose out of my assemblage of notes over the years while reading the Bible. I have simply connected the dots from one amazing revelation to the next, showing the golden thread of clear evidence for a beautiful truth: God created us for Himself. His purposeful guidance for you and me is just as observable as that of a shepherd leading his sheep. In the **Sixty-Six Books of The Mighty Shepherd** narrative, God is the Shepherd of His sheep.

My hope is for you to be wrapped in sheep's clothing as you listen for The Shepherd to call your name, and in so doing you will see with fresh eyes the love He lavishes on His sheep.

Relax and embrace God's desire to join with you in a **covenant relationship.** I believe you will come to know God's marvelous intentions for His people:

His provisions
His protection
His promises
His vision
His instruction
His guidance
His mercy
His forgiveness
His Son

Historically, God spoke to men face-to-face, establishing covenants with Adam, next with Noah, and then with Abraham, Isaac, Jacob, and Moses.

God chose Abraham and made him an extraordinary leader among men because He was intent on establishing through this man a **covenant relationship** with humankind. The New Covenant in Jesus Christ provided us an opportunity that we (in the same way as men of old) may come into a **covenant relationship** through our belief in His blood sacrifice.

When we believe that Jesus Christ was everything God required to reunite and reestablish our rebellious spirits to God, we gain the unmatched privilege of a **covenant relationship** with God.

From the beginning of time, God provided for the people He created, guiding them like a shepherd guides his beloved sheep.
Thus, we have a love story portraying the Mighty Shepherd
who demonstrates His love for us, proclaiming:

I Myself will be the Shepherd of My sheep. —Ezekiel 34:15

As a youngster growing up, I was urged to eat a healthy breakfast. My mother regularly set one of those breakfasts before me, attempting to provide rich nourishment and sustenance that would stick to my ribs.

Much later when I was a wife and a young mother with two children, little time existed to address my personal needs. Happily, spiritual nourishment perched itself on my kitchen counter in the form of a small book entitled *Faith Is . . .* by Pamela Reeves. That little book presented me with a quick but enriching thought—one that "stuck to my ribs" as the day progressed.

My hope in writing **Sixty-Six Books of The Mighty Shepherd** is to set before you spiritual nourishment. Shortened sentences and excerpts from the Bible advance you to rich takeaways in each book. They are emboldened in scripted font and enlarged, enabling you to visually scan the page for immediate truths.

My prayer is for you to experience the golden thread of God's love for you as it weaves throughout the sixty-six books. Taste for yourself the goodness that will "stick to your ribs." Nothing I know of comes closer to fulfilling the hunger within us to be loved than that which God alone can fulfill. It's a life-changing experience to embrace what is revealed in the Bible. His love-messages for you reside in the Bible. Day by day through prayer, reading, and reflection you will continue to experience his love and mercy.

A significant pivotal point in my life was learning how to read the Bible. "*How to*" was as simple yet profound as these three steps:

1. Pray for God to open your mind to what He has for you in his word (the Bible).
2. Read a passage or a chapter—or maybe just a few verses.
3. Ponder the contents; reflect on how and where the words might apply to you.

Because of the Bible's relevance to your life, The Mighty Shepherd will become your soulmate. The results are a *"Me and you"* covenant relationship and a God-guided, God-enriched, God-protected, God-directed life.

I suggest as you read through each "book" of the **Sixty-Six Books of The Mighty Shepherd** with its origin being one of the sixty-six books of the Bible, claim God as The Mighty Shepherd who desires for you to know His care and His compassion. Then cooperate with the fact that He loves you.

May these truths be yours as you read the sixty-six books, knowing God's Word is a lamp to your feet and a light to your path (Psalm 119:105).
It is the Lord who goes before you. He will be with you; He will not fail you or forsake you. Do not fear or be dismayed (Deuteronomy 31:8).

Neither theologian nor scholar,
I'm merely a sheep,
seeking to follow The Mighty Shepherd.
Annette Valentine

I will establish my covenant between

Me and You . . .

Genesis 17:7

It is *the Lord* who goes before you . . .
Deuteronomy 31:8

Book 1
(Origin Genesis)

In the beginning . . .

1:26-28 God created humankind in his own image and blessed them.
2:15-17 The Lord God took the man and put him in the garden of Eden . . .
and commanded him, "You may freely eat of every tree of the garden; but of
the tree of the knowledge of good and evil you shall not eat, for in the day
that you eat of it you shall die."

Countering God's authority was Satan, lying to us:

3:4 "You will not die."

3:6-14 *Humankind broke the covenant* by eating the fruit. In disobedience we denounced God's sovereignty over our lives (paraphrased).

God's command established obedience as a covenant between himself and humankind. But Adam failed to obey, and the consequence imprinted us with a God-challenging nature, making it impossible for us to do what God requires.

3:22-24 As a result, *humankind was expelled,*
and became marked by a fallen nature,
separated from God because of the broken covenant.

6:6-8 And the Lord was sorry that he had made humankind on the earth, and it grieved him to his heart . . . "I am sorry that I have made them."
. . . *But Noah found* favor in the sight of the Lord.

Noah's heart for God prepared the way for God to establish a covenant with him, changing the course of mankind and laying the foundation for new life.

6:18 . . . I will establish my covenant with you; and you shall come into the ark . . .
8:21 I will never again curse the ground because of humankind
. . . for the inclination of the human heart is evil.
9:5 I will surely require a reckoning . . . I will require it from human beings . . .
a reckoning for human life.

9:11-15 *I establish my covenant with you . . .*
never again shall all flesh be cut off by waters . . . and God said,
"This is the sign of the covenant that I make between me and you . . .
for all future generations: I have set my bow in the clouds . . .

I will remember my covenant . . .
between me and you . . ."

This arrangement between God and us was conditional. It came at a cost to be revealed centuries later when God required a sacrificial offering from Abraham. Then, over 400 years passed from the time of Noah until Abraham.

17:1-7 When Abraham was ninety-nine years old, the Lord appeared to him and said, "I am God Almighty; walk before me, and be blameless . . .

I will make my covenant between me and you . . .
and your offspring after you . . . an everlasting covenant . . ."

18:19 ". . . for I have chosen (Abraham) . . . to bring about . . .
what He has promised him."

Through his descendants Abraham was to become the ancestor of a multitude of nations. How then could that be possible when God tested him, requiring a sacrifice of his miracle child, Isaac, whom he fathered at ninety-nine years old? It was when God saw Abraham was prepared to obey that he stopped him from sacrificing his only son.

The place for a required sacrifice stood ready, and Isaac asked,
22:7-8 ". . . but where is the lamb for a burnt offering?" Abraham answered,

"God himself will provide the lamb . . ."

Abraham's near-sacrifice of Isaac is seen as a foreshadowing of Jesus' sacrifice on the cross. The lamb represents Jesus Christ as the "required reckoning" or payment for humankind's disobedience.

BOOK 2
(ORIGIN EXODUS)

MOSES' COVENANT (MOSAIC COVENANT)

2:24 God heard their groaning of his people (in bondage),
and God remembered his covenant . . .
3:4-10 God called to Moses, and Moses answered, "Here I am."
Then God said, "Come no closer! Remove the sandals from your feet,
for the place on which you are standing is holy ground . . .
"I have come to deliver them . . . I will send you . . . I will be with you . . ."
3:11-15 But Moses said to God, "Who am I that I should go to Pharaoh,
and bring the Israelites out of Egypt? . . . what shall I say to them?
. . . and when they ask me (regarding who sent me), 'What is his name?'
3:14-15 . . . God said to Moses,

I Am who I am . . . I am has sent me to you.

4:1 Then Moses answered, "But suppose they do not believe me or listen to me . . ."
4:2 The Lord said to him, "What is that in your hand?" Moses said, "A staff."
4:14-15 The Lord will fight for you; . . . and teach you what you shall do.
4:20 . . . and Moses carried the staff of God in his hand.

19:5 Now therefore, if you obey my voice and keep my covenant,
you shall be my treasured possession . . .
20:2-18 The covenant is the law given to Moses through the Ten Commandments.
29:46 And they shall know that *I am the Lord their God* who brought
them out of the land of Egypt *that I might dwell among them . . .*

Moses's staff had power. It became a snake . . . it parted the seas . . .
Metaphorically, it became the arm of God, leading the people out of bondage.
He carried the staff as an extension of God's own hand, shepherding as one who cares for his sheep.
If you are a shepherd, you need a staff for three reasons.
First, you need it because you're leading the sheep in the countryside and on rocky ground,
so a staff is necessary to help keep you stable. In that sense, it's like a hiking stick.
It catches you when you fall.
The second reason a shepherd needs a staff is for use as an offensive weapon.
If a predator is coming against the sheep, the shepherd can use the staff to fight and defend.
The shepherd's job is to protect the sheep.
A third reason a shepherd would need a staff is because sheep sometimes have minds of their own.
They are not always very smart, and they often wander off. They need correction.
When that happens, a staff can be used to pull them back into the flock and keep the sheep in line.
We can experience that leading, that extension of God's power
to move us in the right direction and away from destruction.

BOOK 3

(ORIGIN LEVITICUS)

20:26 You shall be holy to me; for I the Lord am holy,
and *I have separated you* from the other peoples
to be mine.

26:12-13 *And I will walk among you,*
and will be your God, and you shall be my people.
I am Jehovah your God,
who brought you forth out of the land of Egypt,
to be their slaves no more;

I have broken the bars of your yoke,
and made you walk erect.

Book 4
(Origin Numbers)

3:13 *I consecrated* (you, my people) *for my own . . .*
they shall be mine.
I am the Lord.

We are "God's own," belonging to him who has consecrated us (with synonyms "chosen" and "blessed" further amplifying his love for people). Inherent and unmistakable is the amazing love of the Mighty Shepherd who protects his own.

Similarly, herded sheep rely on shepherds for protection from predators and will stick close to their mother and siblings simply because they are animals that have a strong sense of relatedness. In a large flock, related sheep gather in close proximity and stand together as if to gain an added measure of protection. But sheep are prey animals, and when they are faced with danger, their natural instinct is to flee. After fleeing, sheep will regather in their small familiar groups.

Here we have a glimpse of God's interaction with those he has chosen to rescue and lead, and it is remarkable to recognize God's tenderness toward his beloved. The Old Testament is full of language about the special status of God's chosen people. For example, he refers to them in Book 2 and again in Book 5 as his treasured possessions.

BOOK 5
(ORIGIN DEUTERONOMY)

1:30-31 *The Lord your God, who goes before you*
is the one who will fight for you . . .
the Lord your God carried you,
just as one carries a child, all the way . . .

4:20 *. . . the Lord has taken you and brought you out . . .*
to become . . . his very own possession . . .

7:6 For you are a people holy to the Lord your God;
the Lord your God has chosen you out of all the peoples on earth
to be his people, *his treasured possession.*

7:18-19 . . . do not be afraid . . . *the mighty hand* and
the outstretched arm of the Lord your God has brought you out.

8:2-3 *. . . the Lord your God has led you . . .*
to humble you . . . to know . . . your heart . . . to make you understand . . .

30:19-20 I call heaven and earth to witness against you today
that I have set before you life and death, blessings and curses;
choose life so that you and your descendants may live,
loving the Lord your God, obeying him, and *holding fast to him*;
for that means life to you . . .

31:8 It is *the Lord who goes before you.*
He will be with you; he will not fail you or forsake you.
Do not fear or be dismayed.

32:8-10 When the Most High apportioned the nations,
when he divided humankind . . . the Lord's own portion was his people.
He sustained him in a desert land, in a howling wilderness waste;
he shielded him, cared for him, *guarded him as the apple of his eye.*

BOOK 6
(ORIGIN JOSHUA)

Joshua was Moses' assistant.
Moses had trained him to become his successor.
After Moses died, Joshua had to step up to lead, and
he led Israel as a victorious military commander.
As such, he represents Christ, our captain, the one
who saves us, brings us to the place of rest,
intercedes for us, and makes the conquest over sin possible.

1:1-7 . . . The Lord spoke to Joshua, "My servant Moses is dead.
Now proceed to cross the Jordan, you and all this people, into the land
that I am giving to them . . . Every place that the sole of your foot
will tread upon I have given to you, as I promised Moses.

No one shall be able to stand against you
all the days of your life. As I was with Moses,
so I will be with you; I will not fail you
or forsake you. Be strong and courageous . . ."

1:10-11 Then Joshua commanded: . . . Prepare your provisions . . . for you are to cross over the
Jordan . . . to go in to take possession of the land that the Lord your God gives you to possess.
4:24 . . . so that all the peoples of the earth may know that

The hand of the Lord is mighty . . .

21:43, 45 Thus the Lord gave to Israel all he swore to their ancestors that he would give them.

Not one of all the good promises that the Lord had made
to the house of Israel had failed;
all came to pass.

24:2-13 And Joshua spoke to the people, "Thus says the Lord . . . I took your father Abraham
. . . from beyond the River and led him . . . I gave him Isaac . . . I sent Moses . . . I plagued
Egypt . . . I brought you out . . . I handed them over . . . I destroyed them . . . I would not listen
to the curse of Balaam . . . I rescued you . . . I handed your enemies over to you. It was not by
your sword or by your bow . . . I gave you a land on which you had not labored, and towns you
had not built . . . you eat the fruit of vineyards and olive groves that you did not plant.
24:14-15 Now, therefore revere the Lord, and serve him in sincerity;
put away other gods . . . if you are are unwilling to serve the Lord,

choose this day whom you will serve.

BOOK 7
(ORIGIN JUDGES)

The Book of Judges is a tragic account of how Yahweh (God)
was taken for granted by his children year after year,
century after century. Judges is a sad contrast to the book of Joshua
which chronicles the blessings God bestowed on the
Israelites for their obedience in conquering the land.
In Judges, they were disobedient and idolatrous, leading to their many defeats.
Even so, God has never failed to open his arms in love to his people whenever
they repented from their wicked ways and called upon his name.
The primary message of Judges is that God will not allow
sin to go unpunished. As Exodus established,
Israel was God's people—He was their Shepherd-King.
But they had forsaken the covenant established at Mount Sinai.

2:10 . . . and another generation grew up after them, who did not know the Lord
or the work that he had done . . .
2:18 Whenever the Lord raised up judges for them, *the Lord was* with the judge,
and he *delivered them* from the hand of their enemies all the days
of that judgeship; *for the Lord would be moved to pity*
by their groaning because of those who persecuted and oppressed them.

BOOK 8
(ORIGIN RUTH)

The book of Ruth records tragedy and love in the lives of average people.
Elimelech of Bethlehem with his wife Naomi and their two sons went to
Moab in the time of famine. He and his sons died there.
The wife of one of the sons was Ruth.

1:16 But Ruth said to Naomi, . . .
"Where you go, I will go;
Where you lodge, I will lodge;
your people shall be my people,
and your God my God."

Naomi needed the help of her daughter-in-law to "return to the flock."
Together Ruth and Naomi returned to Naomi's roots, seeking refuge,
and it was in the returning that they were saved.

The social behavior of sheep is dominated by flock mentality.
When the flock leader moves to another pasture, the rest of the flock will follow.
Sheep, however, often go astray, become lost, or otherwise find themselves in need of the shepherd's help to return to the flock. For instance, a sheep that has rolled over onto its back is called a "cast" sheep. Predictably, it may be unable to get up without assistance. This happens most commonly on flat terrain with short, stocky sheep having full fleeces. Heavily pregnant ewes are most prone. Cast sheep can become distressed and die within a short period of time if they are not rolled back into a normal position. When back on their feet, they may need to be supported for a few minutes to ensure they are steady.

2:12 "May the Lord reward you for your deeds, and may you have a full reward from *the Lord, the God of Israel, under whose wings you have come for refuge!"*

4:13-17 So Boaz took Ruth and she became his wife . . . and she bore a son.
. . . They named him Obed; he became the father of Jesse, the father of David.

Boaz was the great-grandfather of David (who became Israel's shepherd-king),
and when Joseph (who was descended from David) married Mary,
their marriage constituted his legal adoption of their son Jesus.

Ruth's act of choosing to seek God's direction actually led to Jesus' life.

BOOK 9
(ORIGIN 1 SAMUEL)

3:1-8 Now the boy Samuel was ministering to the Lord under the priest Eli . . .
Eli perceived that the Lord was calling the boy.
3:19 As Samuel grew up, *the Lord was with him . . .*
4:1 And the word of Samuel came to all Israel.

When Israel was still a relatively young nation, the people became discontent with their lack of a human leader. Part of that notion came from envy of other nations, but there was also a belief that having a human king would make Israel look stronger to potential enemies (the Philistines and others). The elders brought their request for a king to the prophet Samuel.

9:15-16 . . . the Lord had revealed to Samuel: "Tomorrow I will send a man (Saul)
. . . and you shall anoint him to be ruler over my people Israel.
He will save my people from the hand of the Philistines . . ."

15:17-19 Samuel said to Saul, "Though you are little in your own eyes,
are you not the head of the tribes of Israel? *The Lord anointed you king* . . ."
and the Lord sent you on a mission . . .

Why then did you not obey the voice of the Lord . . . ?"
15:23 "For rebellion is no less a sin than divination, and stubbornness . . .
Because you have rejected the word of the Lord, he has also rejected you from being king."

15:24 Saul answered Samuel, "I have sinned; . . . transgressed the commandment of the Lord
and your words, because *I feared the people and obeyed their voice."*
15:26 Samuel said to Saul, "I will not return with you;
for you have rejected the word of the Lord . . ."

Thus, Saul became the king that the people wanted as their leader, but he let his position fill him with an inflated sense of self-importance. Eventually disobedience led to a fracture in Saul's relationship with his Lord and also with Samuel. That division caused the king to experience bouts of depression. Music seemed to soothe Saul, so David was brought into the court because he could play the lute and sing songs for him. David became a trusted member of King Saul's court and later served in his army.

But as David grew in status, the king became jealous when the young man's fame started to overshadow his own. Compromised, he made foolish decisions and chose not to obey the voice of God or that of the person God positioned to instruct him.

Instead, he made the choice to listen to and obey the people whom he was to have been leading.

Ultimately, David replaced Saul as king and became a powerful leader, dependent on God.

30:6 . . . *But David strengthened himself in the Lord his God.*

Book 10

(ORIGIN 2 SAMUEL)

5:12 David then perceived that the Lord had established him king . . .
22:17-20 He reached from on high, he took me, he drew me out of mighty waters.
He delivered me from my strong enemy, from those who hated me;
They came upon me in the day of my calamity, but the Lord was my stay.
He brought me out into a broad place;
he delivered me, because he delighted in me.

22:29-37 Indeed, you are my lamp, O Lord; the Lord lightens my darkness.
By you I can crush a troop, and by my God I can leap over a wall.
This God—his way is perfect; the promise of the Lord proves true;
he is a shield for all who take refuge in him. For who is God, but the Lord?
And who is a rock, except our God?
The God who has girded me with strength has opened wide my path.
He made my feet like the feet of deer, and set me secure on the heights.
He trains my hands for war, so that my arms can bend a bow of bronze.

You have given me the shield of your salvation, and your help has made me great.
You have made me stride freely, and my feet do not slip.

BOOK 11
(ORIGIN 1 KINGS)

2:1-3 When David's time to die drew near, he charged his son Solomon, saying,
"I am about to go the way of all the earth. Be strong, be courageous, and
keep the charge of the Lord your God,
walking in his ways and keeping his statutes . . ."

3:5-9 . . . the Lord appeared to Solomon in a dream and said,
"Ask what I should give you." . . . and Solomon responded:
"I am only a little child; I do not know how to go out or come in.
And your servant is in the midst of the people whom you have chosen,
Give your servant an understanding mind to discern between good and evil . . .

3:10-12 God said to him, ". . . Because
you asked for understanding to discern what is right . . .

Indeed I will give you a wise and discerning mind;
no one like you has been before you and no one like you shall arise after you."

Book 12
(Origin 2 Kings)

Second Kings focuses on the spiritual successes and failures of the two kingdoms of Israel and Judah and continues the story of the kings over these divided kingdoms. It concludes with the final overthrow and deportation of the people of Israel and Judah to Assyria and Babylon, respectively. It explains why Israel and Judah lost the Lord's protection and describes the history of the Northern Kingdom of Israel and the Southern Kingdom of Judah.

The kingdom of Israel was repeatedly ruled by wicked kings. A few of Judah's kings were decent, but the majority of them led the people away from worship of the Lord.

17:7-8 This occurred because the people of Israel had sinned against the Lord their God who had brought them up out of the land of Egypt from under the hand of Pharaoh king of Egypt.

They had worshiped other gods and walked in the customs of the nations . . .

Although a few reigning strong rulers along with God's prophets did exist, they could not stop the nation's decline. The Northern Kingdom of Israel was eventually destroyed by the Assyrians, and about 136 years later the Southern Kingdom of Judah was destroyed by the Babylonians.

BOOK 13
(ORIGIN 1 CHRONICLES)

David was 30 when he became king, and he reigned 40 years.
In Hebron he reigned over Judah seven and a half years,
and in Jerusalem he reigned over all Israel and Judah 33 years.

David's instruction to Solomon who succeeded him as king:

28:9-10 "And you, my son Solomon,
know the God of your father,
and serve him with single mind and willing heart;
for the Lord searches every mind, and understands every plan and thought.

If you seek him, he will be found by you,
but if you forsake him, he will abandon you forever. Take heed now,
for the Lord has chosen you to build a house as the sanctuary;
be strong and act."

Book 14

(Origin 2 Chronicles)

The major focus of Second Chronicles is the reign of Solomon; additionally, the reigns of 20 kings of Judah — from Rehoboam to Zedekiah (approximately 933 to 586 B.C.) — are chronicled. Most importantly, emphasis is on the building and dedication of the temple by King Solomon. His prayer of dedication:

6:12-27 Then Solomon stood before the altar of the Lord . . . spread out his hands . . .
knelt on his knees . . . and said, "O Lord, God of Israel, there is no God like you . . .
you promised . . . and this day have fulfilled . . . Therefore, O Lord, . . .
let your word be confirmed which you promised to your servant David . . .
the place where you promised to set your name . . . heed the prayer . . .
hear the plea . . . hear from heaven . . . hear and forgive.
"When your people Israel, having sinned against you . . . but turn again to you,
and confess your name, and pray and plead . . . may you hear . . . and forgive . . .
teach them the good way in which they should walk . . ."

7:11-14 Thus Solomon finished the house of the Lord . . . then *the Lord said:*
if my people who are called by my name humble themselves,
pray, seek my face, and turn from their wicked ways, then
I will hear from heaven, and will forgive their sin and heal their land.
20:12 . . . We do not know what to do, but our eyes are on you.

BOOK 15
(ORIGIN EZRA)

Ezra, a patriotic Jew, secured permission to return from exile in Babylonia back to Jerusalem and did so. The return of the Israelites to Zion occurred in several waves: those of Sheshbazzar, Zerubbabel, Ezra, and Nehemiah. Ezra described the details of his return and poignantly noted that he refused to ask for armed protection since his trust was in the Lord God.

5:12 But because our ancestors have angered the God of heaven, he gave them
into the hand of King Nebuchadnezzar of Babylon, who destroyed this house
(the temple) and carried away the people to Babylonia . . .
6:1-3 Then King Darius made a decree . . . concerning the house of God at Jerusalem,
let the house be rebuilt . . .
7: 10 For Ezra had set his heart to study the law of the Lord, and to do it, and to teach the
statutes and ordinances in Israel.
7: 28 *I took courage, for the hand of the Lord my God was upon me . . .*
8:31 . . . the hand of our God was upon us, and he delivered us from the hand of the enemy . . .
9:9 *. . . yet our God has extended to us his steadfast love* before the kings of
Persia, *to give us new life* to set up the house of our God,
to repair its ruins, and to give us a wall in Judea and Jerusalem.

BOOK 16

(ORIGIN NEHEMIAH)

In the year 444 B.C., Nehemiah traveled to Israel, leading the third of three returns by the Jewish people following their 70 years of exile in Babylon. (Ezra had led the first two returns.) The return of the Israelites to Zion occurred in several waves: those of Sheshbazzar, Zerubbabel, Ezra, and Nehemiah.

Upon his return, Nehemiah speaks:

1:4-10 When I heard . . . (that the wall of Jerusalem was broken down) . . .
I sat down and wept . . . and prayed: "O Lord God . . . we have offended you deeply.
Remember the word that you commanded your servant Moses,

'If you are unfaithful, I will scatter you . . . but
if you return to me . . . I will gather them . . .'"

Nehemiah affirms God's providence:

2:8 *. . . for the gracious hand of my God was upon me.*

6:15-16 So the wall was finished . . . with the help of our God.

9: 17-24 *. . . you are a God ready to forgive,*
gracious and merciful,
slow to anger and abounding in steadfast love,
and you did not forsake them . . . did not withhold . . .
you sustained them . . .
you gave . . .
you multiplied . . . and brought them out . . .
you subdued (our enemies) . . . and gave them into their hands . . .

9:26 Nevertheless they were disobedient and rebelled against you . . .

9:28-31 *But . . .*
you rescued them according to your mercies . . .
for you are a gracious and merciful God.

BOOK 17
(ORIGIN ESTHER)

The events in the book of Esther occurred during the time period between the first and second of Ezra's efforts to lead the people back to Israel from the Babylonian exile. Evident in the positioning of Esther (a young Jewish woman of Susa) to wed the powerful Persian Emperor Ahasuerus is the unmistakable hand of a sovereign God at work in the lives of his people.

Susa, once the capital of the Persian Empire, is currently made up of three archeological mounds. Atop that archeological site is the modern Iranian town of Shush.

Queen Esther risked her life to save the Jewish people from destruction when the court official Haman persuaded the emperor to authorize a massacre of the entire Jewish population in the empire.

Even today, Esther is said to be the heroine of the Jewish people.

4:14 *. . . Who knows?*
Perhaps you have come . . . for such a time as this?

BOOK 18
(ORIGIN JOB)

1:1 There was once a man . . . whose name was Job.

1:8-11 The Lord said to Satan, "Have you considered my servant Job?
There is no one like him . . . blameless . . . fears God and turns away from evil."
Then Satan answered the Lord, "Does Job fear God for nothing? . . .
stretch out your hand now,
and touch all that he has, and he will curse you to your face."

2:3 The Lord said to Satan regarding Job . . . "He still persists in his integrity,
although you insighted me against him, to destroy him for no reason."

9:24 Job points to (Satan): "The earth is given into the hand of the wicked;
he covers the eyes of its judges—if it is not he, who then is it?"

10:12 Job acknowledges God:

You have granted me life and steadfast love,
and your care has preserved my spirit.

40:10-14 God speaks to Job:
"Deck yourself with majesty and dignity; clothe yourself with glory and splendor.
Pour out the overflowings of your anger,
and look on all who are proud, and abase them . . .
tread down the wicked where they stand . . .

Then I will also acknowledge to you
that your own right hand can give you victory."

42:1-6 Then Job answered the Lord:

"I know that you can do all things,
and that no purpose of yours can be thwarted . . .
therefore I . . . repent . . ."

42:10-12 *And the Lord restored . . . the Lord blessed . . .*

Book 19
(Origin Psalms)

8:4 What are human beings that you are mindful of them,
mortals that you care for them?

16:11 *You show me the path of life.*
In your presence there is fullness of joy . . .

18:2 *The Lord is my rock,* my fortress, and my deliverer, my God . . .
in whom I take refuge, my shield, and the horn of my salvation, my stronghold.

18:19 He brought me out into a broad place;
he delivered me because he delighted in me.
23:1-3 *The Lord is my shepherd,* I shall not want.
. . . he leads me beside still waters; he restores my soul.
He leads me in right paths for his name's sake.
27:5 *He will hide me* in his shelter in the day of trouble;
he will conceal me under the cover of his tent;
he will set me high on a rock.

32:8 *I will instruct you and teach you the way you should go;*
I will counsel you with my eye upon you.

37:23-24 Our steps are made firm by the Lord, when he delights in our way;
though we stumble, we shall not fall headlong,
for the Lord holds us by the hand.

56:9 . . . *This I know, that God is for me.*
56:13 For you have delivered my soul from death, and my feet from falling,
so that I may walk before God in the light of life.
61:2 *From the end of the earth I call to you, when my heart is faint.*
Lead me to the rock that is higher than I.
71:19 . . . You who have done great things, *O God, who is like you?*
73:23-26 . . . you hold my right hand. You guide me with your counsel,
and afterward you will receive me with honor. Whom have I in heaven but you? . . .
My flesh and my heart may fail,
but God is the strength of my heart and my portion forever.

77:19-20 Your way was through the sea, your path, through the mighty waters;
yet your footprints were unseen.
You led your people like a flock . . .

95:7 For he is our God,
and we are the people of his pasture, and the sheep of his hand.

102:18-20 Let this be recorded for a generation to come, so that a people yet
unborn may praise the Lord: that he looked down from his holy height . . .
to hear the groans of the prisoners, to set free those who were doomed to die . . .

105:8 *He is mindful of his covenant forever . . .*

118:6-7 *With the Lord on my side I do not fear.*
What can mortals do to me? The Lord is on my side to help me . . .

119:50 This is my comfort in my distress, that *your promise gives me life.*
119:105 Your word is a lamp to my feet and a light to my path.
119:160 The sum of your word is truth . . .

119:176 *I have gone astray like a lost sheep;* seek out your servant . . .
121:1-3 I lift up my eyes to the hills—from where will my help come?
My help comes from the Lord, who made heaven and earth.
He will not let your foot be moved; he who keeps you will not slumber.

121:5-8 The Lord is your keeper; the Lord is your shade at your right hand.
The sun shall not strike you by day, nor the moon by night.
The Lord will keep you from all evil; he will keep your life.
The Lord will keep your going out
and your coming in from this time on and forevermore.

138:7-8 Though I walk in the midst of trouble, you preserve me . . .
you stretch out your hand, and your right hand delivers me.
The Lord will fulfill his purpose for me;
your steadfast love, O Lord, endures forever. Do not forsake the work of your hands.

139:4-6 Even before a word is on my tongue, O Lord, you know it completely.
You hem me in, behind and before, and lay your hand upon me.
Such knowledge is too wonderful for me; it is so high that I cannot attain it.

143:10 Teach me to do your will, *for you are my God.*
Let your good spirit lead me on a level path.

145:8 *The Lord is gracious and merciful,*
slow to anger and abounding in steadfast love.
145:18 *The Lord is near to all who call on him,*
to all who call on him in truth.
146:3-4 Do not put your trust in princes, in mortals, in whom there is no help.
When their breath departs, they return to the earth;
on that very day their plans perish.

147:10-11 His delight is not in the strength of the horse,
nor his pleasure in the speed of a runner; but the Lord takes pleasure
in those who fear him, in those who hope in his steadfast love.
149:4 *The Lord takes delight in his people;*
he adorns the humble with victory.

BOOK 20
(ORIGIN PROVERBS)

EMPHASIS IN THE PSALMS: God's word sustains and leads us.
EMPHASIS IN PROVERBS: God's wisdom leads us.

3:5-6 *Trust in the Lord with all your heart,*
and do not rely on your own insight. In all your ways
acknowledge him, and he will make straight your paths.

8:22-31 The Lord created me (WISDOM) at the beginning of his work . . .
before the beginning of the earth.
When there were no depths I was brought forth,
when there were no springs abounding with water.
Before the mountains had been shaped, before the hills, I was brought forth—
and he had not yet made earth and fields, or the world's first bits of soil.

(WISDOM continued)

When he established the heavens, I was there,
when he drew a circle on the face of the deep,
when he made firm the skies above,
when he established the fountains of the deep,
when he assigned to the sea its limit,
so that the waters might not transgress his command,
then I was beside him, like a master worker;
and I was daily his delight, rejoicing before him always,
rejoicing in his inhabited world and
delighting in the human race.

16:3 *Commit . . . to the Lord,* and your plans will be established.

16:9 *The human mind plans the way,*
but the Lord directs the steps.

23:18 *Surely there is a future,*
and your hope will not be cut off.

23:26 *My child, give me your heart,*
and let your eyes observe my ways.

Book 21
(Origin Ecclesiastes)

1:4-11 A generation goes, and a generation comes, but the earth remains forever.
The sun rises and the sun goes down, and hurries to the place where it rises.
The wind blows to the south, and goes around to the north;
round and round goes the wind, and on its circuits the wind returns.
All streams run to the sea, but the sea is not full . . .

What has been is what will be,
and what has been done is what will be done;
there is nothing new under the sun . . .

It has already been, in the ages before us.
The people of long ago are not remembered, nor will there be
any remembrance of people yet to come by those who come after them.

In Ecclesiastes we have this direct reminder:
Today is what we are given—
Life it not pointless; it is fleeting! And an urgency exists
to routinely seize joy in our toils as we live it out.

2:24-25 There is nothing better for mortals than to eat and drink,
and find enjoyment in their toil.

This is . . . from the hand of God;
for apart from him who can . . . have enjoyment?

2:26 . . . to the one who pleases him,

God gives wisdom and knowledge and joy . . .

5:20 . . . they will scarcely brood over the days of their lives,
because God keeps them occupied with the joy of their hearts.

8:15 So I commend enjoyment, for there is nothing better for people under the sun . . .
this will go with them in their toil

through the days of life that God gives them . . .

BOOK 22
(ORIGIN SONG OF SOLOMON)

2:16-17 My beloved is mine and I am his;
he pastures his flock among the lilies.
Until the day breathes and the shadows flee . . .

The Song of Solomon alludes to the intimate physical bond one can experience with another human being. God, too, offers a different but very personal relationship. It can be said this book parallels the spiritual oneness God offers. Through the death of his son Jesus, God provided us the way to that relationship.

5:16 *. . . This is my beloved and this is my friend . . .*
8:6-7 *Set me as a seal upon your heart,*
as a seal upon your arm; for love is strong as death . . .
Many waters cannot quench love, neither can floods drown it.

8:13 *. . . listening for your voice . . .*

BOOK 23

(ORIGIN ISAIAH)

9:2 The people who walked in darkness have seen a great light;
those who lived in a land of deep darkness—
on them light has shined.

12:1-3 You will say in that day:
I will give thanks to you, O Lord,
for though you were angry with me, your anger turned away,
and you comforted me.
Surely God is my salvation;

I will trust, and will not be afraid,
for the Lord God is my strength and my might; he has become my salvation.

With joy
you will draw water from the wells of salvation.

19:20 . . . when they cry to the Lord because of their oppressors,
he will send them a savior,
and will defend and deliver them.

26:4 Trust in the Lord forever,
for in the Lord God you have an everlasting rock.

30:21 And when you turn to the right or when you turn to the left,
your ears shall hear a word behind you saying,
"This is the way; walk in it."

30:29-30 *You shall have a song . . . and gladness of heart . . .*
And the Lord will cause his majestic voice to be heard . . .

35:3-8 Strengthen the weak hands, and make firm the feeble knees.
Say to those who are of a fearful heart,

"Be strong, do not fear! Here is your God . . ."

Then the eyes of the blind shall be opened, and the ears of the deaf unstopped;
then the lame shall leap like a deer, and the tongue of the speechless sing for joy.
For waters shall break forth in the wilderness, and streams in the desert . . .

A highway shall be there,
and it shall be called the Holy Way . . .

40:1-2 Comfort, O comfort my people, says your God.
Speak tenderly to Jerusalem, and cry to her
that she has served her term . . . her penalty is paid . . .

40:11 *He will feed his flock like a shepherd;*
he will gather the lambs in his arms,
and carry them in his bosom . . .

40:26 . . . calling them all by name . . .

40:28-31 . . . *The Lord is the everlasting God,*
the Creator of the ends of the earth.
He does not faint or grow weary;
his understanding is unsearchable.

He gives power to the faint,
and strengthens the powerless.

Even youths will faint and be weary, and the young will fall exhausted; but

those who wait for the Lord shall renew their strength,
they shall mount up with wings like eagles,
they shall run and and not be weary,
they shall walk and not faint.

41:10 . . . *do not fear, for I am with you, do not be afraid,*
for I am your God;

I will strengthen you, I will help you,
I will uphold you with
my victorious right hand.

42:6 I am the Lord,
I have called you in righteousness,
I have taken you by the hand and kept you . . .

42:16 . . . *I will turn the darkness before them into light,*
the rough places into level ground . . .

43:1-5 But now thus says the Lord, he who created you . . . he who formed you . . .
Do not fear, for I have redeemed you;
I have called you by name, you are mine.
For I am the Lord your God . . . your Savior . . .
you are precious in my sight, and honored, and I love you . . .
Do not fear, for I am with you . . .
43:10-11 . . . so that you may know and believe me and understand that I am he.
Before me no god was formed, nor shall there be any after me.
I, I am the Lord, and besides me there is no savior.
44:22 I have swept away your transgressions like a cloud, and your sins like a mist;
return to me, for I have redeemed you.
45:2-3 I will go before you and level the mountains,
I will break in pieces the doors of bronze and cut through the bars of iron,
I will give you the treasures of darkness and riches hidden in secret places,
so that you may know that it is I,
the Lord, the God of Israel, who calls you by your name.
45: 22 *Turn to me and be saved . . .*
For I am God, and there is no other.
46:4 . . . even to your old age I am he, even when you turn gray I will carry you.
I have made, and I will bear; I will carry and will save.

52:1-2 Awake, awake, put on your strength, O Zion! . . .
Shake yourself from the dust, rise up, O captive Jerusalem;
loose the bonds from your neck, O captive daughter Zion!
52:12 For you shall not go out in haste, and you shall not go in flight;
the Lord will go before you,
and the God of Israel will be your rear guard.
54:6 For the Lord has called you . . .

54:8 . . . *with everlasting love I will have compassion on you,*
says the Lord, your redeemer.

54:10. . . the mountains may depart and the hills be removed, but my steadfast love
shall not depart from you, and my covenant of peace shall not be removed,
says the Lord, who has compassion on you.
55:12-13 For you shall go out in joy, and be led back in peace; the mountains and the
hills before you shall burst into song, and all the trees of the field shall clap their hands.
Instead of the thorn shall come up the cypress;
instead of the brier shall come up the myrtle; and it shall be to the Lord for a memorial,
for an everlasting sign that shall not be cut off.

58:8-11 Then your light shall break forth like the dawn,
and your healing shall spring up quickly; your vindicator shall go before you,
the glory of the Lord shall be your rear guard.

Then you shall call, and the Lord will answer;
you shall cry for help, *and he will say, Here I am . . .*
then your light shall rise in the darkness and your gloom be like the noonday.
The Lord will guide you continually,
and satisfy your needs in parched places,
and make your bones strong . . .
you shall be like a watered garden,
like a spring of water, whose waters never fail.

60:1-5 Arise, shine; for your light has come,
and the glory of the Lord has risen upon you . . .
Then you shall see and be radiant;
and your heart shall thrill and rejoice . . .

60:17-20 . . . I will appoint Peace as your overseer and Righteousness as your taskmaster . . .
but the Lord will be your everlasting light, your God will be your glory.
62:2-5 *. . . and you shall be called by a new name*
that the mouth of the Lord will give.

You shall be a crown of beauty in the hand of the Lord,
and a royal diadem in the hand of your God.
You shall no more be termed Forsaken,
and your land shall no more be termed Desolate; but

you shall be called My Delight Is in Her . . .
for the Lord delights in you . . .
and as the bridegroom rejoices over the bride, so shall your God rejoice over you.

63:9 . . . It was no messenger or angel but his presence that saved them;
in his love and in his pity he redeemed them;
he lifted them up and carried them all in the days of old.

BOOK 24
(ORIGIN JEREMIAH)

1:5 "Before I formed you in the womb I knew you, and
before you were born I consecrated you . . ."

3:15 *I will give you shepherds after my own heart,*
who will feed you with knowledge and understanding.

3:19 I thought how I would set you among my children, and give you a pleasant land,
the most beautiful heritage of all the nations. And
I thought you would call me, My Father,
and would not turn from following me.

11:10 *They . . . have broken the covenant*
that I made with their ancestors.
13:11 . . . I made (them) cling to me, says the Lord,
in order that they might be for me a people, a name, a praise, and a glory.
But they would not listen.

14:9 . . . *Yet you, O Lord, are in the midst of us,*
and we are called by your name;
do not forsake us!

15:16 . . . *your words became to me a joy and*
the delight of my heart;
for I am called by your name . . .

24:7 I will give them a heart to know that I am the Lord;
and they shall be my people
and I will be their God,
for they shall return to me with their whole heart.

29:11-13 *. . . surely I know the plans I have for you,*
says the Lord, plans for your welfare and not for harm,
to give you a future with hope.
Then when you call upon me and come and pray to me, I will hear you.
When you search for me you will find me; if you seek me with all your heart.

31:3 *. . . I have loved you with an everlasting love;*
therefore I have continued my faithfulness to you . . .

31:31-34 *. . . I will make a new covenant . . .*
I will put my law within them,
and I will write it on their hearts; and I will be their God,
and they shall be my people . . .
I will forgive their iniquity, and remember their sin no more.
32:40-41 I will make *an everlasting covenant* with them . . .
I will rejoice in doing good to them,
and I will plant them in this land in faithfulness, with all my heart and all my soul.

33:14-16 *The days are surely coming, says the Lord,*
when I will fulfill the promise
I made to the house of Israel
and the house of Judah.

In those days and at that time
I will cause a righteous Branch to spring up for David;

and he shall execute justice and righteousness in the land.
In those days Judah will be saved and Jerusalem will live in safety.

And this is the name by which it will be called:
"The Lord is our righteousness."

Book 25

(ORIGIN LAMENTATIONS)

3:21-24 But this I call to mind and therefore I have hope:

the steadfast love of the Lord never ceases,
his mercies never come to an end;
they are new every morning;
great is your faithfulness.

"The Lord is my portion," says my soul,
"therefore I will hope in him."

Book 26

(ORIGIN EZEKIEL)

34:11-16 For thus says the Lord God:

I myself will search for my sheep, and will seek them out.
As shepherds seek out their flocks
when they are among their scattered sheep,
so I will seek out my sheep. I will rescue them
from all the places to which they have been scattered on a day
of clouds and thick darkness.
I will bring them out from the peoples and gather them from the countries,
and will bring them into their own land;
I will feed them on the mountains of Israel,
by the watercourses, and in all the inhabited parts of the land.
I will feed them with good pasture,
and the mountain heights of Israel shall be their pasture; there they shall lie down
in good grazing land, and they shall feed on rich pasture on the mountains of Israel.
I myself will be the shepherd of my sheep, and . . . I will seek the lost,

I will bring back the strayed, and I will bind up the injured . . .

34:25-31 *I will make with them a covenant of peace . . .*
I will make them and the region around my hill a blessing;
and I will send down the showers in their season;
they shall be showers of blessing.
The trees of the field shall yield their fruit, and the earth shall yield its increase.
They shall be secure on their soil;
and *they shall know that I am the Lord,* when I break the bars
of their yoke, and save them from the hands of those who enslaved them . . .

You are my sheep, the sheep of my pasture
and I am your God . . .

36:26-27 *A new heart I will give you,*
and a new spirit I will put within you;
and I will remove from your body the heart of stone and give you a heart of flesh.
I will put my spirit within you . . .

47:12 *. . . because the water for* (you) *flows from the sanctuary.*

BOOK 27
(ORIGIN DANIEL)

Daniel was among the first group of Jewish captives taken to Babylon by King Nebuchadnezzar in 605 B.C. His apocalyptic vision foretold the rise and fall of four world empires, along with the rise and permanence of God's eternal and universal kingdom.

The name Daniel means "God is my judge," and in the ensuing events of this book, Daniel's stance before King Nebuchadnezzar amplifies God's direct intervention in the actions of his people.

Daniel speaks—

2:37-45 . . . "You, O King . . . After you shall arise another kingdom inferior to yours . . .
a divided kingdom . . . they will not hold . . . And in the days of those kings
the God of heaven will set up a kingdom
that shall never be destroyed,
nor shall this kingdom be left to another people.
It shall crush all these kingdoms and bring them to an end, and it shall stand forever,

3:16-18 . . . we have no need to present a defense to you in this matter (O King) . . .
our God whom we serve is able to deliver us . . .
. . . we will not serve your gods . . .

6:3 Soon Daniel distinguished himself . . . because an excellent spirit was in him . . .
6:22-27 My God sent his angel and shut the lions' mouths
so that they would not hurt me . . .

for he is the living God, enduring forever . . .
He delivers and rescues,

he works signs and wonders . . .

DANIEL'S PROMISE-CLAIMING PRAYER:

9:3-19 Then I turned to the Lord God . . . "All Israel has transgressed . . .
refusing to obey your voice . . . Incline your ear, O my God . . .
We do not present our supplication before you
on the ground of our righteousness, but on the ground of your great mercies.

O Lord, hear; O Lord, forgive . . .
because . . . your people bear your name!"

10:18-19 Again one in human form touched me and strengthened me.
He said, *"Do not fear, greatly beloved, you are safe.*
Be strong and courageous!"

Book 28
(Origin Hosea)

1:10 . . . and in the place where it was said to them, "You are not my people,"
it shall be said to them, *"Children of the living God."*
6:1-3 *"Come, let us return to the Lord . . .*
he will raise us up, that we may live before him . . .
he will come to us like the showers, like the spring rains that water the earth."

11:2-4 The more I called to them, the more they went from me . . .
Yet it was I . . . *I took them up in my arms;*
but they did not know that I healed them.
I led them with cords of human kindness,
with bands of love.
I was to them like those who lift infants to their cheeks.
I bent down to them and fed them.

12:6 But as for you,
return to your God,
hold fast to love and justice,
and wait continually for your God.

14:4-7 I will heal their disloyalty;
I will love them freely,
for my anger has turned from them . . .
They shall again live beneath my shadow,
they shall flourish as a garden;
they shall blossom like the vine,
their fragrance shall be like the wine of Lebanon.

BOOK 29

(ORIGIN JOEL)

2:1 *. . . the day of the Lord is coming . . .*

2:12-13 . . . even now, says the Lord,

return to me with all your heart . . .
Return to the Lord, your God,
for he is gracious and merciful,
slow to anger,
and abounding in steadfast love . . .

Book 30
(Origin Amos)

2:4 *. . . they have been led astray*
by the same lies after which their ancestors walked.

3:12 Thus says the Lord:
As the shepherd rescues
from the mouth of the lion two legs, or a piece of an ear,
so shall the people of Israel . . . be rescued . . .

9:11-12 *On that day I will raise up* . . . and repair . . . and rebuild . . .
in order that they may possess . . . and
all the nations who are called by my name,
says the Lord who does this.

9:15 *I will plant them upon them upon their land,*
and they shall never again be plucked up out of the land
that I have given them, says the Lord your God.

BOOK 31
(ORIGIN OBADIAH)

1:21 *Those who have been saved*
shall go up to Mount Zion . . .
and the kingdom shall be the Lord's.

BOOK 32
(ORIGIN JONAH)

1:1-3 Now the word of the Lord came to Jonah . . .
But Jonah set out to flee . . . from the presence of the Lord.

1:17 But the Lord provided a large fish to swallow up Jonah . . .

2:1-2 Then Jonah prayed to the Lord his God . . . saying,
"I called to the Lord out of my distress,
and he answered me . . .

2:7-9 As my life was ebbing away, I remembered the Lord;
and my prayer came to you, into your holy temple.
Those who worship vain idols forsake their true loyalty . . .
Deliverance belongs to the Lord!"

BOOK 33
(ORIGIN MICAH)

5:4-5 *And he shall stand and feed his flock*
in the strength of the Lord, in the majesty of the name of the Lord his God.
And they shall live secure,
for now he shall be great . . . and he shall be the one of peace.

6:5 *". . . remember . . .*
that you may know the saving acts of the Lord."

6:8 He has told you, O mortal, what is good; and
what does the Lord require of you but to do justice,
and to love kindness, and to walk humbly with your God?

7:7 But *as for me, I will look to the Lord,*
I will wait for the God of my salvation; my God will hear me.
7:8 Do not rejoice over me, O my enemy;
when I fall, I shall rise;
when I sit in darkness, the Lord will be a light to me.

BOOK 34
(ORIGIN NAHUM)

1:7-9 *The Lord is good, a stronghold in a day of trouble;*
he protects those who take refuge in him,
even in a rushing flood.

He will make a full end of his adversaries, and will pursue his enemies into darkness.

Why do you plot against the Lord? . . .

1:15 *Look!*
On the mountains the feet of one who brings good tidings,
who proclaims peace!

Book 35
(Origin Habakkuk)

1:5 *. . . a work is being done in your days*
that you would not believe if you were told.
2:3 *For there is still a vision for the appointed time;*
it speaks of the end, and does not lie.
If it seems to tarry, wait for it; it will surely come . . .

2:20 *. . . the Lord is in his holy temple;*
let all the earth keep silence before him!

3:17-19 Though the fig tree does not blossom, and no fruit is on the vines;
though the produce of the olive fails and the fields yield no food;
though the flock is cut off from the fold and there is no herd in the stalls,

yet I will rejoice in the Lord;
I will exult in the God of my salvation.

God, the Lord, is my strength;
he makes my feet like the feet of a deer,
and makes me tread upon the heights.

BOOK 36
(ORIGIN ZEPHANIAH)

3:14-17 Sing aloud, O daughter Zion; shout, O Israel!
Rejoice and exult with all your heart, O daughter Jerusalem!
The Lord has taken away the judgments against you,
he has turned away your enemies.

The king of Israel, *the Lord, is in your midst;*
you shall fear disaster no more.
On that day it shall be said to Jerusalem:
Do not fear, O Zion; do not let your hands grow weak.
The Lord, your God, is in your midst, a warrior who gives victory;
he will rejoice over you with gladness,
he will renew you in his love;
he will exult over you with loud singing . . .

Book 37
(ORIGIN HAGGAI)

2:4-8 . . . take courage, all you people of the land, says the Lord . . .
for I am with you . . .
according to the promise that I made you
when you came out of Egypt.

My spirit abides among you; do not fear . . .
Once again in a little while, I will shake the heavens and the earth
and the sea and the dry land; and I will shake all the nations, so that
the treasure of all nations shall come,
and I will fill this house with splendor,
says the Lord of hosts.

BOOK 38

(ORIGIN ZECHARIAH)

2:7-8 For thus said the Lord of hosts . . . :

Truly, one who touches you touches the apple of my eye.

8:12-15 . . . *For there shall be a sowing of peace;*
the vine shall yield its fruit, the ground shall give its produce,
and the skies shall give their dew;
and I will cause the remnant of this people to possess all these things . . .
I will save you and you shall be a blessing.
Do not be afraid, but let your hands be strong . . . again
I have purposed in these days to do good . . .

9:11-12 *As for you also,*
because of the blood of my covenant with you,
I will set your prisoners free from the waterless pit.
Return to your stronghold, O prisoners of hope;
today I declare that I will restore to you double.

10:2-5 *. . . people wander like sheep;*
they suffer for lack of a shepherd . . .
the Lord of hosts cares for his flock,
. . . and will make them like his proud war horse.

Out of them shall come the cornerstone, out of them the tent peg,
out of them the battle bow, out of them every commander.
Together they shall be like warriors in battle,
trampling the foe in the mud of the streets; they shall fight,
for the Lord is with them . . .

10:12 *I will make them strong in the Lord,*
and they shall walk in his name, says the Lord.

BOOK 39
(ORIGIN MALACHI)

3:7 Ever since the days of your ancestors
you have turned aside . . .

Return to me,
and I will return to you,
says the Lord of hosts . . .

THE NEW COVENANT

of

OUR LORD AND SAVIOR JESUS CHRIST

BOOK 40

(ORIGIN MATTHEW, an apostle of Jesus Christ, written A.D. 50-60)

1:16 . . . *Jesus was born, who is called the Messiah.*

4:16 *". . . the people who sat in darkness*
have seen a great light,
and for those who sat in the region and shadow of death
light has dawned."

4:19 *And he said to them,*
"Follow me . . ."

9:27-28 As Jesus went on from there . . .
(they) followed him, crying *"Have mercy on us . . ."*
Jesus said to them,
"Do you believe that I am able to do this?"
They said to him, "Yes, Lord."

11:25-29 Jesus said . . .

"Come to me,

all you that are weary and are carrying heavy burdens,

and I will give your rest.

Take my yoke upon you, and learn from me,

for I am gentle and humble in heart,

and you will find rest for your souls . . ."

13:16 ". . . blessed are your eyes, for they see, and your ears, for they hear."

BOOK 41

(ORIGIN MARK, an apostle of Jesus Christ, written as early as A.D. 50)

4:11 And he (Jesus) said to them,

"To you has been given
the secret of the kingdom of God . . ."

6:34 . . . and

he had compassion for them,
because they were like sheep without a shepherd . . .

8:29 He asked them,

"But who do you say that I am?" . . .

Photo by Jeff LaGro
photoartbypicard.com

BOOK 42

(ORIGIN LUKE, an apostle of Jesus Christ, written approximately A.D. 60)

4:16-21 When he (Jesus) came to Nazareth, where he had been brought up,
he went to the synagogue on the sabbath day, as was his custom.
He stood up to read, and the scroll of the prophet Isaiah was given to him.
He unrolled the scroll and found the place where it was written:

"The Spirit of the Lord is upon me, because
he has anointed me
to bring good news to the poor.
He has sent me to proclaim release to the captives
and recovery of sight to the blind,
to let the oppressed go free,
to proclaim the year of the Lord's favor."

And he rolled up the scroll, gave it back to the attendant, and sat down.
The eyes of all in the synagogue were fixed on him. Then he began to say to them,
"Today this scripture has been fulfilled in your hearing."

11:9-10 *"So I say to you,*
Ask, and it will be given you;
search, and you find;
knock, and the door will be opened for you.
For everyone who asks receives,
and everyone who searches finds,
and for everyone who knocks,
the door will be opened . . ."

BOOK 43

(ORIGIN JOHN, an apostle of Jesus Christ, written A.D. 90-95)

1:16-17 From his fullness we have all received, grace upon grace. The law indeed was given through Moses; grace and truth came through Jesus Christ.
1:38 When Jesus turned and saw them following, he said to them,

"What are you looking for?"

3:16-18 "For God so loved the world that he gave his only Son, so that everyone who believes in him may not perish but may have eternal life . . . God did not send the Son into the world to condemn the world, but in order that the world might be saved through him. Those who believe in him are not condemned . . ."

5:6-9 When Jesus saw him lying there and knew that he had been there a long time, he said to him,

"Do you want to be made well?"

The sick man answered him, "Sir, I have no one to put me into the pool when the water is stirred up; and while I am making my way, someone else steps down ahead of me." Jesus said to him,

"Stand up, take your mat and walk."

At once the man was made well, and he took up his mat and began to walk.

5:25 “Very truly, I tell you, the hour is coming, and is now here,
when the dead will hear the voice of the Son of God, and those who hear will live . . .”

8:11 . . . *And Jesus said, “Neither do I condemn you . . .”*
8: 31-32 Then Jesus said . . . “If you continue in my word, you are truly my disciples;
and you will know the truth, and the truth will make you free.”

10:2-11 “. . . The one who enters by the gate is the shepherd of the sheep.
The gatekeeper opens the gate for him,
and the sheep hear his voice.
He calls his own sheep by name and leads them out.
When he has brought out all his own, he goes ahead of them,
and the sheep follow him because they know his voice . . .

. . . *"I am the gate for the sheep . . .*

Whoever enters by me will be saved,
and will come in and go out and find pasture.
The thief comes only to steal and kill and destroy.

I came that they may have life, and have it abundantly.
I am the good shepherd.

The good shepherd lays down his life for his sheep . . ."

10:27-28 . . . "My sheep hear my voice. I know them, and they follow me.
I give them eternal life, and they will never perish.
No one will snatch them out of my hand . . ."

14:1-6 "Do not let your hearts be troubled. Believe in God, believe also in me. In my Father's house there are many dwelling places. If it were not so, would I have told you that I go to prepare a place for you? And if I go and prepare a place for you, I will come again and will take you to myself, so that where I am, there you may be also . . .

I am the way, and the truth, and the life.
No one comes to the Father except through me . . ."

14:27 ". . . Peace I leave with you; my peace I give to you. I do not give to you as the world gives. Do not let your hearts be troubled, and do not let them be afraid . . ."
17:13 *". . . and I speak these things in the world so that they may have my joy made complete in themselves . . ."*

20:30-31 Now Jesus did many other signs in the presence of his disciples, which are not written in this book. But these are written so that you may come to believe that Jesus is the Messiah, the Son of God, and that through believing you may have life in his name.

BOOK 44

(ORIGIN ACTS of the apostles, written somewhere between A.D. 64 and 72)

1:1-8 . . . I (Luke, an apostle) wrote about all that Jesus did and taught from the beginning until the day when he was taken up to heaven, after giving instructions through the Holy Spirit to the apostles whom he had chosen. After his suffering he presented himself alive to them by many convincing proofs, appearing to them over the course of forty days and speaking about the kingdom of God. While staying with them, he ordered them not to leave Jerusalem, but to

wait there for the promise of the Father.

"This," he said, "is what you have heard from me; for John baptized with water, but

you will be baptized with the Holy Spirit

not many days from now . . .

you will receive power

when the Holy Spirit has come upon you . . ."

2:22-28 (Peter, an apostle, speaks.) “You that are Israelites,
listen to what I have to say: Jesus of Nazareth, a man attested to you by God
with deeds of power, wonders, and signs that God did through him among you,
as you yourselves know—this man, handed over to you according to the definite plan
and foreknowledge of God,

you crucified and killed by the hands of those outside the law.

But God raised him up, having freed him from death,

because it was impossible for him to be held in its power. For (King) David says
concerning him, *‘I saw the Lord always before me,*

for he is at my right hand so that I will not be shaken;

therefore my heart was glad,

and my tongue rejoiced;

moreover my flesh will live in hope.

For you will not abandon my soul to Hades, or let your Holy One experience corruption.

You have made know to me the ways of life;

you will make me full of gladness with your presence.’

13:26-41 (Paul, an apostle after the original twelve apostles, speaks.)
"My brothers, you descendants of Abraham's family, and others who fear God,

to us the message of this salvation has been sent . . .
and we bring you good news

that what God promised to our ancestors he has fulfilled for us, their children,
by raising Jesus . . .
Let it be known to you therefore, my brothers,
that through this man forgiveness of sins is proclaimed to you;

by this Jesus everyone who believes is set free

from all those sins from which you could not be freed by the law of Moses . . ."

17:22-28 Then Paul said, "... From one ancestor he made all nations to inhabit the whole earth, and he allotted the times of their existence and the boundaries of the places where they would live, so that they would

search for God

and perhaps grope for him and find him

—though indeed he is not far from each one of us.

For 'In him we live and move and have our being' ..."

26:4-30 (Paul defending himself before King Agrippa, claiming Jesus' calling:) ... 'I am sending you to

open their eyes

so that they may turn from darkness to light

and from the power of Satan to God,

so that they may receive forgiveness

of sins and a place among those who are sanctified by faith in me.'

BOOK 45

(ORIGIN ROMANS, Paul's letter to them in A.D. 55-56)

1:1-6 Paul, a servant of Jesus Christ, called to be an apostle, set apart for
the gospel of God . . . we have received grace . . . including yourselves who are
called to belong to Jesus Christ,

8:1-6 *There is therefore now no condemnation*
for those who are in Christ Jesus.
For the law of the Spirit of life in *Christ Jesus has set you free*
from the law of sin and of death. For God has done what the law, weakened
by the flesh, could not do: by sending his own Son in the likeness of sinful flesh,
and to deal with sin, he condemned sin in the flesh so that the just requirement
of the law might be fulfilled in us, who walk not according to the flesh,
but according to the Spirit . . .
to set the mind on the Spirit is life and peace.

8:14-17 For all who are led by the Spirit of God are children of God . . .

you did not receive a spirit of slavery to fall back in to fear,

but you have received a spirit of adoption.

When we cry, "Abba! Father!" it is that very Spirit bearing witness with our spirit that

we are children of God,

and if children, then heirs, heirs of God . . ."

9:16 So it depends not on human will or exertion, but on God who shows mercy.

13:11-14 Besides this, you know what time it is, how it is now the moment for you to

wake from sleep . . .

the night is far gone, the day is near . . .

put on the armor of light . . .

put on the Lord Jesus Christ.

15:13 May the God of hope fill you with all joy and peace in believing,
so that you may abound in hope by the power of the Holy Spirit.

BOOK 46

(ORIGIN 1 CORINTHIANS, Paul's letter to them in A.D. 55)

1:27-31 But God . . . is the source of your life in

Christ Jesus, who became for us wisdom from God,
and righteousness and sanctification and redemption . . .

2:5 . . . so that your faith might rest not on human wisdom but on the power of God.

2:9 . . . as it is written, *"What no eye has seen,*
nor ear heard, nor the human heart conceived,
what God has prepared for those who love him" –

6:17-20 . . . anyone united to the Lord becomes one spirit with him . . .
do you not know that your body is a temple of the Holy Spirit within you,
which you have from God, and that . . .

you were bought with a price . . .

15:57 *. . . thanks be to God, who gives us the victory*
through our Lord Jesus Christ.

BOOK 47

(ORIGIN 2 CORINTHIANS, Paul's letter to them around 56 A.D.)

3:15-18 Indeed, to this very day whenever Moses is read,
a veil lies over their minds; but

when one turns to the Lord, the veil is removed.

Now the Lord is the Spirit,

and where the Spirit of the Lord is, there is freedom.

And all of us, with unveiled faces . . . are being transformed into the same image
from one degree of glory to another; for this comes from the Lord, the Spirit.
5:17-18 *So if anyone is in Christ, there is a new creation:*
everything old has passed away; see,

everything has become new!

All this is from God, who reconciled us to himself through Christ . . .
6:16 . . . For we are the temple of the living God; as God said,

I will live in them and walk among them,
and I will be their God, and they shall be my people . . ."

13:5 Examine yourselves to see whether you are living in faith. Test yourselves.

Do you not realize that Jesus Christ is in you? . . .

BOOK 48

(ORIGIN GALATIANS, Paul's letter to them 52 A.D.)

1:15-16 But when *God, who had set me apart*
before I was born
and called me through his grace,
was pleased to reveal his Son to me . . .

3:13-14 *Christ redeemed us*
from the curse of the law by becoming a curse for us — for it is written,
"Cursed is everyone who hangs on a tree" — in order that in Christ Jesus
the blessing of Abraham might come to the Gentiles,
so that we might receive the promise
of the Spirit through faith.

4:28 *Now you, my friends, are children of the promise . . .*

Book 49

(ORIGIN EPHESIANS, Paul's letter to them 60-61 A.D.
Ephesians is one of four "prison epistles" written during Paul's captivity
—also Colossians, Philippians, and Philemon.)

1:3-8 Blessed be the God and Father of our Lord Jesus Christ . . .
He destined us for adoption as his children through Jesus Christ . . .
In him we have redemption through his blood,
the forgiveness of our trespasses, according to the riches of his
grace that he lavished on us . . .

1:17-18 I pray . . . that, with the eyes of your heart enlightened, you may
know what is the hope to which he has called you,
what are the riches of his glorious inheritance . . .

2:4-10 But God, who is rich in mercy, out of the great love with which
he loved us even when we were dead through our trespasses,
made us alive together with Christ —
by grace you have been saved —

and raised us up with him and seated us with him in the heavenly places
in Christ Jesus,

so that in the ages to come
he might show the immeasurable riches of his grace
in kindness toward us in Christ Jesus.

For by grace you have been saved through faith, and this is not your own doing;

it is the gift of God

— not the result of works, so that no one may boast.
For we are what he has made us, created in Christ Jesus for good works,
which God prepared beforehand to be our way of life.
2:13-14 But now in Christ Jesus (by the blood of Christ)

you who once were far off have been brought near.
For he is our peace . . .

and has broken down the dividing wall, that is, the hostility between us.

3:16-19 I pray that, according to the riches of his glory,
he may grant that you may

be strengthened in your inner being with power
through his Spirit, and
that Christ may dwell in your hearts through faith . . .

I pray that you may have the power to comprehend, with all the saints,
what is the breadth and length and height and depth, and to

know the love of Christ that surpasses knowledge,
so that you may be filled with all the fullness of God.

4:14-15 . . . no longer be children, tossed to and fro and blown about by every wind of doctrine, by people's trickery, by their craftiness in deceitful scheming . . . grow up in every way into him who is the head, into Christ.

5:14 . . . for everything that becomes visible is light. Therefore it says,

"Sleeper, awake!
Rise from the dead, and Christ will shine on you."

BOOK 50

(ORIGIN PHILIPPIANS, Paul's letter to them 60-61 A.D.
— one of four "prison epistles")

2:7-11 . . . And being found in human form,
he (Jesus Christ) humbled himself and became obedient
to the point of death—even death on a cross.
Therefore God also highly exalted him and gave him
the name that is above every name,
so that at the name of Jesus every knee should bend,
in heaven and on earth and under the earth,
and every tongue should confess that Jesus Christ is Lord,
to the glory of God the Father.

2:12-13 . . . work out your own salvation . . .
for it is God who is at work in you . . .

3:12-14 *. . . because Christ Jesus has made me his own . . .*
this one thing I do: forgetting what lies behind and
straining forward to what lies ahead,

I press on toward the goal for the prize
of the heavenly call of God in Christ Jesus.

4:6-7 Do not worry . . . but in everything by prayer and supplication
with thanksgiving let you requests be made known to God.
And the peace of God, which surpasses all understanding,
will guard your hearts and your minds in Christ Jesus.

4:19 *. . . God will fully satisfy every need of yours*
according to his riches in glory in Christ Jesus.

Book 51

(Origin Colossians, Paul's letter to them between 60-61 A.D.—
one of four "prison epistles")

1:19-20 For in him (Jesus Christ) . . . and through him

God was pleased to reconcile to himself all things,
. . . by making peace through the blood of his cross.

2:13-14 And when you were dead in trespasses . . .

God made you alive together with him, when he forgave us . . .
erasing the record that stood against us . . .

2:18-19 *Do not let anyone disqualify you*

. . . (grow) with a growth that is from God.

3:2 Set your minds on things that are above . . .

3:12-16 *. . . clothe yourselves with compassion*
. . . Above all, clothe yourselves with love,
which binds everything together in perfect harmony.
And let the peace of Christ rule in your hearts . . .
Let the word of Christ dwell in you richly . . .

BOOK 52

(ORIGIN 1 THESSALONIANS, Paul's letters to them between 50-51 A.D.)

1:4-10 For we know, brothers and sisters beloved by God, that

he has chosen you . . . and how

you turned to God

from idols, to serve a living and true God . . .

to wait for his Son from heaven,

whom he raised from the dead — Jesus, who rescues us . . .

2:11-12 . . . like a father with his children, urging and encouraging you . . .

(to) lead a life worthy of God, who calls you into his own kingdom and glory.

5:9-10 *For God has destined us not for wrath*

but for obtaining salvation through our Lord Jesus Christ,

who died for us . . .

5:16-21 *Rejoice always, pray without ceasing,*

give thanks in all circumstances;

for this is the will of God in Christ Jesus for you. Do not quench the Spirit.

Do not despise the words of prophets, but

test everything; hold fast to what is good . . .

BOOK 53

(ORIGIN 2 THESSALONIANS)

2:13-15 . . . *because God chose you . . .*
he called you . . .

that you may obtain the glory of our Lord Jesus Christ.
So then, brothers and sisters,
stand firm and hold fast . . .

3:3 . . . *the Lord is faithful;*
he will strengthen you and guard you . . .

3:16 Now may the Lord of peace himself give you peace at all times in all ways.
The Lord be with all of you.

BOOK 54

(ORIGIN 1 TIMOTHY. Paul's three letters—1 Timothy, 2 Timothy, and Titus—
are know as the Pastorals, written to his younger colleagues in the early 60s A.D.)

2:5-6 *For there is one God;*
there is also one mediator between God and humankind,
Christ Jesus,
himself human, who gave himself a ransom for all . . .

6:11-12 But as for you . . . pursue righteousness, godliness, faith,
love, endurance, gentleness. Fight the good fight of the faith;
take hold of the eternal life to which you were called . . .
6:20-21 *. . . guard what has been entrusted to you.*
Avoid the profane chatter and contradictions of what is falsely called knowledge;
by professing it some have missed the mark . . .
Grace be with you.

BOOK 55

(ORIGIN 2 TIMOTHY)

3:12-17 Indeed, all who want to live a godly life in Christ Jesus will be persecuted.
But wicked people and imposters will go from bad to worse, deceiving others and
being deceived. But as for you, continue in what you have learned and firmly
believed, knowing from whom you learned it, and how from childhood you have
known the sacred writings (the Bible, Scripture, God's Word) that are able to
instruct you for salvation through faith in Christ Jesus.

All scripture is inspired by God (God-breathed)
and is useful for teaching, for reproof, for correction,
and for training in righteousness,
so that everyone who belongs to God may be proficient,
equipped for every good work.

4:17 *But the Lord stood by me and gave me strength,*
so that through me the message might be fully proclaimed . . .

BOOK 56
(ORIGIN TITUS)

2:7-8 Show yourself in all respects a model of good works, and in your teaching show integrity, gravity, and sound speech that cannot be censured . . .
2:11 *For the grace of God has appeared,*
bringing salvation to all . . .

3:4-7. . . when the goodness and loving kindness of God our Savior appeared,
he saved us,
not because of any works of righteousness that we had done,
but according to his mercy,
through the water of rebirth and renewal by the Holy Spirit.
This Spirit he poured out on us richly through Jesus Christ our Savior,
so that, having been justified by his grace,
we might become heirs according to the hope of eternal life.

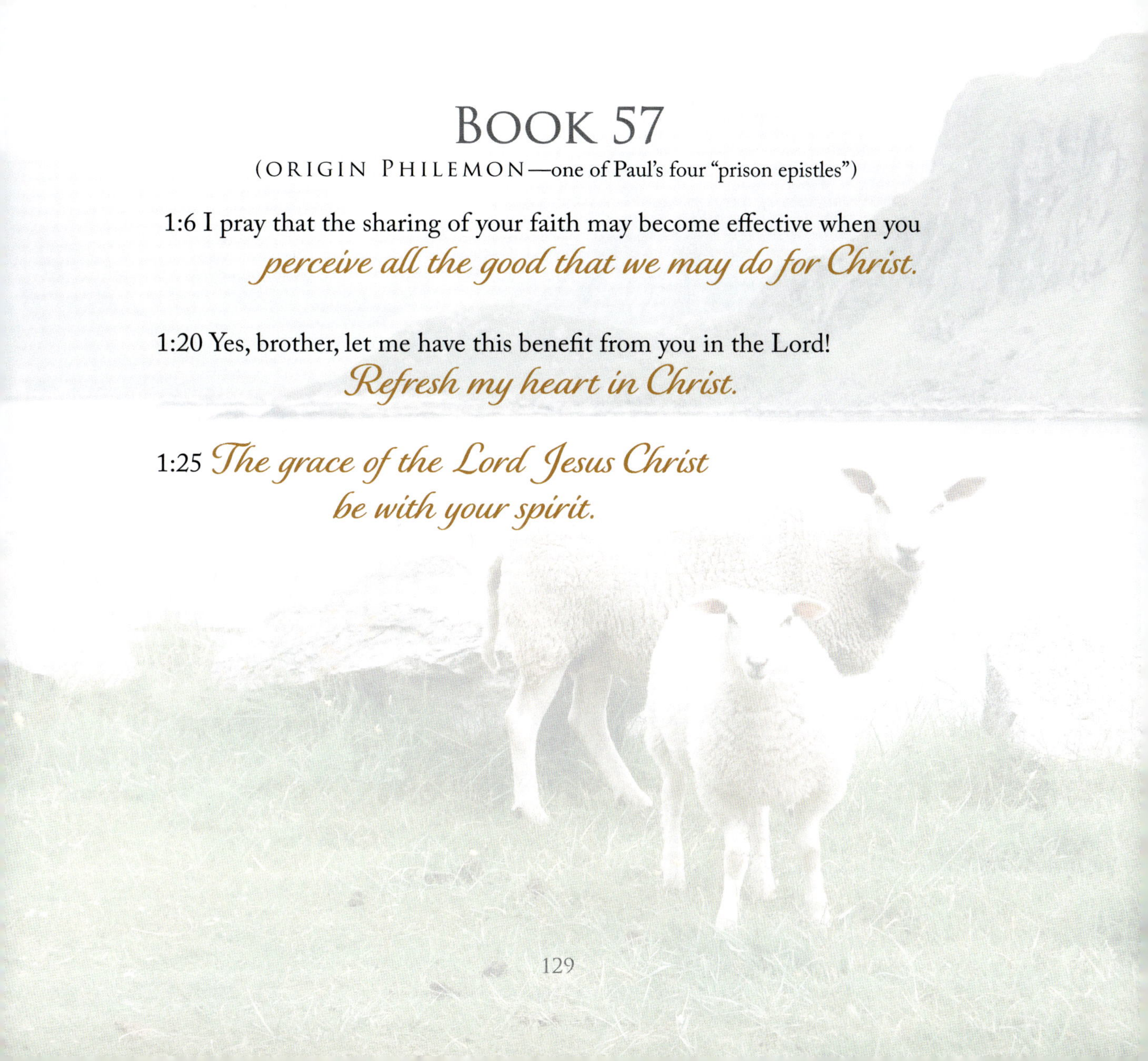

BOOK 57

(ORIGIN PHILEMON—one of Paul's four "prison epistles")

1:6 I pray that the sharing of your faith may become effective when you *perceive all the good that we may do for Christ.*

1:20 Yes, brother, let me have this benefit from you in the Lord! *Refresh my heart in Christ.*

1:25 *The grace of the Lord Jesus Christ be with your spirit.*

BOOK 58

(ORIGIN HEBREWS)

(This letter came from the second-generation era of Christians, probably 70 A.D.)

3:7-8 Therefore, as the Holy Spirit says,
"Today, if you hear his voice, do not harden your hearts . . ."
4:16 Let us therefore approach the throne of grace with boldness,
so that we may receive mercy
and find grace to help in time of need.
6:17-20 In the same way, when God desired to show even more clearly
to the heirs of the promise the unchangeable character of his purpose,
he guaranteed it by an oath, so that through two unchangeable things,
in which it is impossible that God would prove false,
we who have taken refuge might
be strongly encouraged to seize the hope set before us.
We have this hope,
a sure and steadfast anchor of the soul,
a hope that enters the inner shrine behind the curtain, where Jesus,
a forerunner on our behalf, has entered, having become a high priest forever . . .

7:18-19 There is . . . the introduction of

a better hope, through which we approach God.

7:22-27 *. . . Jesus has also become*

the guarantee of a better covenant . . .

he is able for all time to save those who approach God through him . . .

For it was fitting that we should have such a high priest,

holy, blameless, undefiled, separated from sinners, exalted above the heavens.

Unlike the other high priests, he has no need to offer sacrifices day after day . . .

this he did once for all when he offered himself.

8:6 . . . Jesus . . . is the mediator of a better covenant . . .

8:8-12 *"The days are surely coming, says the Lord,*

when I will establish a new covenant . . .

This is the covenant that I will make . . . says the Lord:

I will put my laws in their minds, and write them on their hearts,

and I will be their God, and they shall be my people . . .

For I will be merciful toward their iniquities,

and I will remember their sins no more."

9:11-14 *But when Christ came . . .*
he entered once for all into the Holy Place,
not with the blood of goats and calves, but
with his own blood, thus obtaining eternal redemption . . .
. . . how much more will the blood of Christ . . . purify our conscience
. . . to worship the living God!
9:15 *For this reason he is the mediator of a new covenant,*
so that those who are called may receive the promised eternal inheritance, because
a death has occurred that redeems them . . .
9:22 . . . without the shedding of blood there is no forgiveness of sins.
9:26-28 . . . he has appeared once for all at the end of the age to remove sin
by the sacrifice of himself . . . having been offered once to bear the sins of many . . .

10:16-18 "This is the covenant that I will make . . . says the Lord: I will put my laws
in their hearts . . ." . . . he also adds, "I will remember their sins . . . no more."
Where there is forgiveness of these,
there is no longer any offering for sin.

10:23 Let us hold fast to the confession of our hope without wavering,
for he who has promised is faithful.

12:1-2 . . . let us also lay aside every weight and the sin that clings . . .
let us run with perseverance the race that is set before us,
looking to Jesus
the pioneer and perfecter of our faith, who for the sake of the joy that was
set before him endured the cross, disregarding its shame,
and has taken his seat at the right hand of the throne of God.
12:12-13 Therefore *lift your drooping hands*
and strengthen your weak knees,
and make straight paths for your feet,
so that what is lame may not be put out of joint, but rather be healed.
12:18-24 *You have not come to something that can be touched . . .*
But you have come to Mount Zion
and to the city of the living God . . .
and to Jesus, the mediator of a new covenant . . .

BOOK 59

(ORIGIN JAMES, written between 45 and 50 A.D.)

1:1 James, a servant of God and of the Lord Jesus Christ . . .

4:5 . . . do you suppose that it is for nothing that the scripture says,

"God yearns jealously
for the spirit that he has made to dwell in us?"

4:7-8 Summit yourselves therefore to God. Resist the devil,
and he will flee from you.

Draw near to God, and he will draw near to you . . .

4:10 *Humble yourselves before the Lord,*
and he will exalt you.

5:8 You also must be patient.

Strengthen your hearts,
for the coming of the Lord is near.

BOOK 60

(ORIGIN 1 PETER, a letter of living hope in the midst of suffering from Peter at Rome to believers prior to his martyrdom around 65—67 A.D.)

1:3-5 Blessed be the God and Father of our Lord Jesus Christ!

By his great mercy he has given us a new birth
into a living hope through the resurrection of Jesus Christ

. . . into an inheritance that is imperishable, undefiled, and unfading,

kept in heaven for you . . .
protected by the power of God . . .

1:8-9 Although you have not seen him, you love him; and even though you do not see him now, you believe in him and rejoice with an indescribable and glorious joy,

for you are receiving the outcome of you faith,
the salvation of your souls.

1:13 Therefore prepare your minds for action; discipline yourselves;
set all your hope on *the grace that Jesus Christ will bring you when he is revealed.*

1:18-19 *You know that you were ransomed . . .*
with the precious blood of Christ . . .

1:23-25 *You have been born anew . . .*
of imperishable seed, through the living and enduring word of God.

For "All flesh is like grass . . . (it) withers and the flower falls, but
the word of the Lord endures forever."
That word is the good news that was announced to you.

2:9-10 But you are . . . God's own people . . . called . . . out of darkness
into his marvelous light. Once you were not a people,
but now you are God's people; *once you had not received mercy,*
but now you have received mercy.

2:24-25 He himself bore our sins in his body on the cross, so that, free from sins,
we might live for righteousness; *by his wounds you have been healed.*
For you were going astray like sheep,
but now you have returned to the shepherd
and guardian of your souls.

BOOK 61

(ORIGIN 2 PETER, written at Rome about 65-67 A.D.)

1:3-4 *His divine power has given us*
everything needed for life and godliness,
through the knowledge of him who called us by his own glory and goodness.
Thus he has given us . . .
his precious and very great promises . . .
1:19 So we have *the prophetic message*
more fully confirmed. You will do well to be attentive to this as to
a lamp shining in a dark place,
until the day dawns
and the morning star rises in your hearts.

3:17-18 You therefore, beloved, since you are forewarned, beware that you
are not carried away with the error of the lawless and lose you own stability.
But grow in the grace and knowledge
of our Lord and Savior Jesus Christ.
To him be the glory both now and to the day of eternity.
Amen.

BOOK 62

(ORIGIN 1 JOHN. Tradition has associated John with this and the next two letters, the same John the apostle who wrote the Gospel of John and later Revelation.)

1:5-7 *God is light and in him there is no darkness at all.*
If we say that we have fellowship with him while we are walking in darkness,
we lie and do not do what is true; but
if we walk in the light as he himself is in the light,
we have fellowship with one another,
and the blood of Jesus his Son cleanses us from all sin.

2:12 I am writing to you, little children, because
your sins are forgiven on account of his name.
2:20 But *you have been anointed by the Holy One . . .*

3:8 . . . The Son of God was revealed for this purpose . . .
4:4 Little children, *you are from God,* and have conquered them;
for the one who is in you is greater than the one who is in the world.

5:4-5 *. . . And this is the victory that conquers the world, our faith.*
Who is it that conquers the world but the one who believes that Jesus is the Son of God?

Book 63
(Origin 2 John)

1:2-3 . . . because of

the truth that abides in us and will be with us forever:

Grace, mercy, and peace will be with us from
God the Father and from Jesus Christ, the Father's Son,
in truth and love.

Book 64
(Origin 3 John)

1:2 *Beloved, I pray*
that all may go well with you
and that you may be in good health, just as
it is well with your soul.

BOOK 65

(ORIGIN JUDE, the brother of James, the leader of the Jerusalem church.
In MARK 6:3 both of them are called brothers of Jesus.)

1:20-21 But you, beloved, build yourselves up on your most holy faith;
pray in the Holy Spirit;

keep yourselves in the love of God;
look forward to the mercy of our Lord Jesus Christ
that leads to eternal life.

1:24-25 *Now to him who is able to keep you from falling,*
and to make you stand without blemish
in the presence of his glory with rejoicing,
to the only God our Savior,
through Jesus Christ our Lord,
be glory, majesty, power, and authority,
before all time and now and forever.
Amen.

BOOK 66

(ORIGIN REVELATION to John from God. The book closes the canon of Scripture. The closing of the canon means there is no new revelation given to us by God.)

2:10 . . . *be faithful until death,*
and I will give you the crown of life.

3:3 Remember then what you received and heard; obey it, and repent.
If you do not wake up, I will come like a thief, and
you will not know at what hour I will come to you.

3:8 . . . *Look, I have set before you an open door,*
which no one is able to shut . . .

3:20 *Listen! I am standing at the door, knocking;*
if you hear my voice and open the door,
I will come in to you and eat with you, and you with me.

4:8 And the four living creatures, each of them with six wings,
are full of eyes all around and inside. Day and night
without ceasing they sing,

"Holy, holy, holy, the Lord God the Almighty,
who was and is and is to come."

4:10-11 . . . they cast their crowns before the throne, singing,

"You are worthy, our Lord and God,
to receive glory and honor and power,
for you created all things,
and by your will they existed and were created."

5:9-10 They sing a new song:
"You are worthy to take the scroll and to open its seals,
for you were slaughtered
and by your blood
you ransomed for God saints
from every tribe and language and people and nation;

you have made them to be a kingdom and priests serving our God,
and they will reign on earth."

5:11-12 Then I looked, and I heard the voice of many angels
surrounding the throne and the living creatures and the elders;
they numbered myriads of myriads and thousands of thousands,
singing with full voice,
"Worthy is the Lamb that was slaughtered
to receive power and wealth and wisdom and might
and honor and glory and blessing!"

7:14-17 Then he said to me, "These are they who have come out
of the great ordeal; they have washed their robes and made them
white in the blood of the Lamb.

For this reason they are before the throne of God . . .
and the one who is seated on the throne will shelter them.

They will hunger no more, and thirst no more; the sun will not strike them,
nor any scorching heat;

for the Lamb at the center of the throne
will be their shepherd,
and he will guide them
to springs of the water of life,
and God will wipe away every tear from their eyes."

If your heart longs for a shepherd, consider praying this simple prayer, acknowledging your desire and need for a Savior:

> Lord, I have turned from you, and I am lost.
> I believe your Son is reaching out in love to me
> and has paid the price for all my sins.
> I invite you to come into my heart,
> and I rejoice that you have
> embraced me as your own.

Joseph Newton Hadden (circa 1925, Todd County, Kentucky) with his prize-winning New Hampshire sheep

EPILOGUE

LEGACY drives home a point for me: I came from a bloodline that is undeniable. My father is my father. Nothing can change that fact about him or me. We will forever be related to each other. The same is true of his relationship with his father. Many circumstances can separate, but the father and son or father and daughter relationship continues.

I barely knew him, but I love this photo of my paternal grandfather because I see something wonderful in him: a humbled position, the likeness of a shepherd kneeling so that he can embrace his prized possession. In my most vidid memory, Papa Joe treated me with humility and kindness, so much so that it follows I sense a very real thread of similarity between God the Father's love for me—His child—and the legacy that has enabled me to come to know God's love and sacrifice. The Shepherd lays down His life for His sheep.

It has been an extreme joy for me to highlight from the Bible the countless and immeasurable acts through which God humbled Himself to show us His shepherding ways, using covenants, and prophets, and His Word, and chosen leaders-apostles, and His Holy Spirit to personally lead His sheep. And when we have become His Own, He calls us by that Spirit to shepherd others . . .

It would be impossible for me to disregard the three special people who have been my staying power, encouraging me, bolstering me, holding me accountable, and (yes) pestering me to get to the finish line with my vision for this book. My deepest gratitude to my daughter Jenifer Valentine Hofmann, my dear Elktonian "sister" and first editor Carolyn L. Wells, and my illustrious and very patient book designer Eve DeGrie.

Annette Hadden Valentine
www.annettehvalentine.com

About the Author

Annette Valentine is author of the engaging and inspirational trilogy entitled *My Father*, a series that will leave you hungering for a fourth book. "Who knows?" she says with a delightfully serious note. "They're each spirited sagas that focus on the deep love of a father for his child, and that, my friend, is a never-ending story! So perhaps there will be an upcoming fourth in the series." *Eastbound from Flagstaff* was her award-winning debut novel, and *Down to the Potter's House* is the second in the series. *Sufficient Sacrifice* is the third.

Her writing began with a knack for believing in spine-tingling ghost stories and Nancy Drew mysteries. At the heart of this creative and intensely energetic writer is her purposeful compassion that launched an advocacy of the anti-human trafficking movement.

Annette is a graduate of Purdue University and a retired professional interior designer having enjoyed a gratifying 34-year career. As a way to continue sharing beauty and good design, Annette owns Valentine House, a unique gift boutique in Franklin, Tennessee. She lives near Nashville with her husband Walt. They have two grown children, six grandchildren, and a beloved Boxer named Heidi.

To learn more about the author and receive a sampling of the Study Guide, and her work, scan the QR code or visit her website: **www.annettehvalentine.com**